Wild Baby Animals

FIRST EDITION
Series Editor Deborah Lock; **US Senior Editor** Shannon Beatty;
Project Art Editor / Illustrator Charlotte Jennings; **Art Director** Martin Wilson;
Senior Producer, Pre-Production Nikoleta Parasaki;
Reading Consultant Linda Gambrell, PhD

THIS EDITION
Editorial Management by Oriel Square
Produced for DK by WonderLab Group LLC
Jennifer Emmett, Erica Green, Kate Hale, *Founders*

Editors Grace Hill Smith, Libby Romero, Michaela Weglinski;
Photography Editors Kelley Miller, Annette Kiesow, Nicole DiMella; **Managing Editor** Rachel Houghton;
Designers Project Design Company; **Researcher** Michelle Harris; **Copy Editor** Lori Merritt;
Indexer Connie Binder; **Proofreader** Larry Shea; **Reading Specialist** Dr. Jennifer Albro;
Curriculum Specialist Elaine Larson

Published in the United States by DK Publishing
1745 Broadway, 20th Floor, New York, NY 10019

Copyright © 2023 Dorling Kindersley Limited
DK, a Division of Penguin Random House LLC
23 24 25 26 10 9 8 7 6 5 4 3 2
002-333979-June/2023

All rights reserved.
Without limiting the rights under the copyright reserved above, no part of this publication may be reproduced, stored in or introduced into a retrieval system, or transmitted, in any form, or by any means (electronic, mechanical, photocopying, recording, or otherwise), without the prior written permission of the copyright owner.
Published in Great Britain by Dorling Kindersley Limited

A catalog record for this book
is available from the Library of Congress.
HC ISBN: : 978-0-7440-7292-1
PB ISBN: 978-0-7440-7293-8

DK books are available at special discounts when purchased in bulk for sales promotions, premiums,
fundraising, or educational use. For details, contact: DK Publishing Special Markets,
1745 Broadway, 20th Floor, New York, NY 10019
SpecialSales@dk.com

Printed and bound in China

The publisher would like to thank the following for their kind permission to reproduce their images:
a=above; c=center; b=below; l=left; r=right; t=top; b/g=background

Getty Images: 500px / Joni Hidayat 13bl; **Getty Images / iStock:** graphicphoto 19;
naturepl.com: Danny Green 20-21, Sebastian Kennerknecht 21crb, Andy Rouse 24b, Shattil & Rozinski 17b;
Shutterstock.com: Diana Taliun 10cb, Sergey Uryadnikov 29b
Cover images: *Front:* **Dreamstime.com:** Roomyana b/g, Pojanee Yotasiri clb; *Back:* **Shutterstock.com:** Hangouts Vector Pro cra, cla

All other images © Dorling Kindersley
For more information see: www.dkimages.com

For the curious
www.dk.com

Level 2

Wild Baby Animals

Deborah Lock

Contents

6	Squirrels
8	Rabbits
10	Kangaroos
12	Silvered Leaf Monkeys
14	Bears
16	Foxes
18	Deer
20	Sea Otters
22	Giraffes
24	Elephants
26	Gorillas
28	Crocodiles
30	Glossary
31	Index
32	Quiz

Squirrels

Squirrel pups are born in a warm and cozy nest.

They have no fur and their eyes are closed.

zzz!

newborn pups

squirrel pup

juvenile squirrel

They start to climb at eight weeks old.

Rabbits

Rabbit kits are born deep inside burrows.

They drink their mom's milk for the first few weeks.

By one month old, they spend most of their time outside.

newborn rabbit kit

rabbit kit

young rabbit

Kangaroos

At birth, a kangaroo joey is the size of a jelly bean.

The joey crawls up its mom's fur and falls into her pouch.

newborn joey

The joey spends more than six months in the pouch.

wriggle!

Silvered Leaf Monkeys

An infant silvered leaf monkey has bright orange fur.

It spends all day in the trees.

It takes about six months for its fur to change color.

infant silvered leaf monkey

juvenile silvered leaf monkey

adult silvered leaf monkey

Bears

Bear cubs are born in twos or threes.

blink!

blink!

A bear gives birth in a den in midwinter.

In spring, the cubs peek out for the first time.

Bears are mammals. Most mammals give birth to live babies.

Foxes

Furry fox cubs are wide-eyed and hear very well.

There are many sights and sounds for them to explore.

They jump around and practice their pouncing skills.

Deer

A baby deer is called a fawn. It runs and leaps on long, nimble legs.

But when it senses danger, the fawn curls up and hides in leaves.

Its speckled pattern makes the fawn hard to see.

Sea Otters

A sea otter needs to swim and dive to find food.

But sea otter pups don't know how to swim when they're born.

splash!

The otter pup has thick fur so it can float on the ocean's surface. Its mother will find food for a few months until the pup grows its adult fur. Then, the pup will learn to swim.

Giraffes

A baby giraffe
is called a calf.
It can walk just an hour
after being born.

stretch!

The calf learns to use its long neck to reach up high to nibble leaves.

It spends as much as 18 hours a day eating.

Elephants

An elephant calf
sucks its trunk
like a human baby
sucks its thumb.

spray

The calf then learns to use its trunk to wash and drink.

It finds out its trunk can pull up plants and be used for lots of other things.

Gorillas

Infant gorillas stay with their moms for three years.

munch

They learn to pick fruit and leaves, and munch on stalks and roots.

Infants also learn to build nests out of plants.

27

Crocodiles

Crocodile hatchlings learn to hunt very quickly.

They are born knowing how to swim and how to catch small animals.

Crocodiles are reptiles that lay eggs. The babies then grow and hatch out of their eggs as hatchlings.

They keep getting bigger until one day they are grown up.

Goodbye, baby animals!

Glossary

Burrow
A hole that leads to an underground home with tunnels

Hatch
To break out of a shell

Mammals
A group of animals that are warm-blooded, have backbones, and are covered in fur or hair

Nibble
To take small bites of food

Pounce
To suddenly jump or swoop onto something

Reptile
An animal with dry, scaly skin that lives on land

Speckled
Covered with small spots of color

Index

bears 14–15
burrow 8
crocodiles 28–29
deer 18
den 15
elephants 24–25
fawn 18
foxes 16–17
giraffes 22–23

gorillas 26–27
hatchlings 28–29
joey 10–11
kangaroos 10–11
mammals 15
monkeys 12–13
nest 6, 27
otters 20–21
pouch 10, 11

pouncing 17
rabbits 8–9
reptiles 29
sea otters 20–21
silvered leaf monkeys 12–13
squirrels 6–7
swimming 20, 21, 28
trunk 24, 25

31

Quiz

Answer the questions to see what you have learned. Check your answers in the key below.

1. What is a baby kangaroo called?
2. What does a fawn do when it senses danger?
3. How does a sea otter pup stay safe before it can swim?
4. What are three things that an elephant calf can do with its trunk?
5. How many hours a day does a baby giraffe spend eating?

1. A joey 2. It curls up and hides 3. The pup has thick fur that makes it float 4. Wash itself, drink, and pull up plants 5. As much as 18 hours a day